ASK THE
CONSTITUTION

Can States Make Their Own Laws?

Alex Acks

Enslow Publishing
101 W. 23rd Street
Suite 240
New York, NY 10011
USA

enslow.com

Published in 2020 by Enslow Publishing, LLC.
101 W. 23rd Street, Suite 240, New York, NY 10011

Library of Congress Cataloging-in-Publication Data

Names: Acks, Alex, author.
Title: Can states make their own laws? / Alex Acks.
Description: New York : Enslow Publishing, 2020. | Series: Ask the constitution | Audience: Grades 5–8. | Includes bibliographical references and index.
Identifiers: LCCN 2018048043| ISBN 9781978507128 (library bound) | ISBN 9781978508415 (pbk.)
Subjects: LCSH: Exclusive and concurrent legislative powers—United States. |Federal government—United States. | Constitutional law—United States. | Interstate relations—United States.
Classification: LCC KF4600 .A93 2019 | DDC 342.73/042—dc23
LC record available at https://lccn.loc.gov/2018048043

Printed in the United States of America

To Our Readers: We have done our best to make sure all website addresses in this book were active and appropriate when we went to press. However, the author and the publisher have no control over and assume no liability for the material available on those websites or on any websites they may link to. Any comments or suggestions can be sent by email to customerservice@enslow.com.

Contents

Introduction

State laws have always governed marriage in the United States.[1] But in 1996, the Defense of Marriage Act (DOMA) was signed by President Bill Clinton and became the law for the whole country. Section 3 of DOMA stated that even if states allowed same-sex couples to marry, the government of the United States wouldn't recognize those marriages—and other states didn't have to either.[2] That meant, for example, if a same-sex couple got married in Vermont (which allowed those marriages starting in 2009[3]) and then moved to Texas, their new home state wouldn't recognize they were married. Same-sex couples were barred from receiving federal benefits other married couples could have, such as social security if one spouse died. When DOMA passed, same-sex marriages weren't legal in any of the states. A court ruling in Hawaii in 1993 brought up the possibility.[4] In 2013, Bill Clinton himself urged the Supreme Court to overturn the law.[5]

Why did Bill Clinton change his mind in 2013? Three related court cases heading for the Supreme Court of the United States (SCOTUS) aimed squarely at Section 3 of DOMA: *Massachusetts v. Department of Health and Human Services,*[6] *Gill v. Office of Personnel Management,*[7] and *United States v. Windsor.*[8] *Gill* and *Windsor* attacked DOMA from the angle of the equal protection clause in the Fifth Amendment to the Constitution.[9, 10] In his ruling on *Massachusetts v. Department of Health and Human Services,* district court judge Tauro said, "**DOMA plainly intrudes on a core area of** state sovereignty—the ability to define the marital status of its citizens—also convinces this court that the statute violates the Tenth Amendment."[11]

The Tenth Amendment to the Constitution states, "The powers not delegated to the United States by the Constitution, nor prohibited by it to the States, are reserved to the States respectively, or to the people."[12] In other words, powers that aren't specifically given to the United States government by the Constitution belong to the states.[13] In *Massachusetts v. Department of Health and Human Services*, Judge Tauro said that because the Constitution doesn't specifically give the government the power to decide the definition of marriage, it can't tell the states how *they* have to define it.

Only *United States v. Windsor* was heard by the Supreme Court—because they only needed to decide one case. On June 26, 2013, married same-sex couples in thirteen states and Washington, DC,[14] (and anyone with ambitions of being married some day!) had a reason to celebrate. The Supreme Court of the United States made a 5–4 decision that Section 3 of DOMA violated the equal protection clause of the Constitution.

The push and pull over who gets to make the laws, the states or the US government, and whose laws will win when the two are in conflict, is ongoing and ever-changing. In this book, we'll explore the history and some of the complicated relationships of state versus national law, an endless war fought in courtrooms and real battlefields.

1

The Need for a Constitution

After the Second Continental Congress adopted the Declaration of Independence on July 4, 1776, the thirteen colonies faced more problems than just a war with Great Britain. If there was a chance that the war for independence would succeed, they needed to form their own government. This government would run the army that would fight the war, would engage in diplomacy with other countries to get help, and would make sure a functioning country survived at the end. The Americans needed to figure out how laws would be made and who would make them.

The Constitution of the United States of America has been the governing document of our country since it was approved on June 21, 1788. There's an almost twelve-year gap between the thirteen colonies declaring independence and the start of the United States as we know it. What happened during those years?

The Articles of Confederation

The Second Continental Congress took up the issue of forming a new government immediately after the Declaration was signed. Debate started on July 22, 1776, and was combative, particularly on issues such as if voting

This 1977 United States postage stamp commemorates the drafting of the Articles of Confederation, two hundred years afterward.

should be proportional or state-by-state.[1] Another more difficult issue was how much power the new central government would have.

Among the many reasons the colonists rebelled against Great Britain was a feeling that the authority of the far-off British government was overbearing and tyrannical. It isn't a surprise that when it came time to put together a new government, many delegates of the Second Continental Congress didn't want a strong central government.[2] An earlier attempt at a united colonial government in 1754, called the Albany Plan of Union, failed because the individual colonies didn't want to give up any power.[3] Over twenty years later, the governing bodies of the individual colonies still wanted to keep as much power to themselves as they could. There were also concerns among the delegates that a republic wouldn't work for a country as big as the one they were trying to form; the delegates would be too far removed from the people.[4]

This is believed to be the first political cartoon—made by Benjamin Franklin. It shows the colonies as a snake, divided into segments that cannot live on their own.

As a prelude to the ugliest fight in the later creation of the Constitution, there was conflict over taxation, with John Dickinson of Delaware pushing for taxes proportional to all residents of a state, both free and enslaved. The southern states demanded that only white inhabitants should be counted.[5] (Later, when the states started devaluing their land to avoid paying taxes, the Confederation Congress again tried to set up a tax related to population, with enslaved people counting as three-fifths of a free person. That tax effort never passed the Congress, but "three-fifths" would continue to haunt the United States, as we'll see in chapter 3.[6])

After over a year of debate, in October of 1777, the Articles of Confederation were sent to the new states for ratification. The articles were a compromise that kept the central government as weak as possible and imagined a country that was a loose group of sovereign states—though it would still be called "The United States of America"[7] when fully ratified in 1779.

Failures and Accomplishments of the Confederation Congress

The confederation government had extremely limited powers. The government could conduct foreign diplomacy, regulate the army and postal service, make and borrow money, and conduct war. These powers were even more limited because the Confederation Congress had no enforcement power.[8] States went around the Congress several times to negotiate with foreign powers; for example, the state of Georgia pursued its own foreign policy with the Spanish when it came to the territory of Florida.[9]

The government couldn't raise taxes, either. Only states could do that—and then the government could request money from the states. The states rarely provided the money they were asked for.[10] Among other problems, this led to soldiers in the Continental Army not being paid, resulting in at least one mutiny—the Pennsylvania Line Mutiny.[11]

While the failures of the Articles of Confederation were many and resounding, they provided the United States with the government it needed to survive the Revolutionary War. They proved that forming a government by means of a Constitutional Convention *could* work. The Second Continental Congress, under the Articles of Confederation, also wrote and adopted the Northwest Ordinance of 1787. The Northwest Ordinance of 1787 was created to deal with land west of the original thirteen colonies (modern-day Illinois, Indiana, Ohio, Michigan, and Wisconsin[12]). It established rules for how the land should be divided and admitted to the union as states. It also guaranteed certain rights for the people of those territories, including religious freedom and criminal rights, like trial by jury.[13] As the United States grew, the Northwest Ordinance of 1787 was renewed and recycled for the admission of new states, long after the government that had created it ceased to exist.[14]

By 1786, less than ten years after it started, the weak government created by the Articles of Confederation led a disintegrating union of states, lacking the power to execute its most basic functions. If the United States of America were going to survive, there needed to be some big changes.

"Not Worth a Continental"

Under the Articles of Confederation, the Congress could coin money and issue bills of credit, but it lacked the authority to keep the states from also issuing bills of credit and money. There was no coordination between the two. Neither the national government nor the states took bills out of circulation. The British also carried out a campaign of economic warfare by making fake Continental bills. Because of this, the value of the "Continentals" dropped immensely—there were too many of them, causing depreciation. By 1780, they were worth 1/40 of their face value—that's like if you had $10 and it was only worth $0.25. That's where the saying, "Not worth a Continental" came from.[15]

George Washington, Benjamin Franklin, and others are shown at the signing of the Constitution in 1787.

The Constitutional Convention

With a clear view of what had gone wrong with the Articles of Confederation—too much power in the states and the need for a stronger central government—the Constitutional Convention began in May 1787. For the next five months, representatives from each of the states argued, debated, and compromised to create the document that is still the basis for our government: the United States Constitution.

The changes from the Articles of Confederation were profound. The new Constitution created a strong national government in three branches: executive, judicial, and legislative. Each was intended to provide checks and balances on the others as a means to keep the government from abusing its new power.[16]

The new Constitution was sent to the states to be ratified; by the summer of 1788, eleven of the thirteen states had ratified it. On September 13, 1788, the Confederation Congress voted to implement the new Constitution. The government as Americans had known it would end on the first Wednesday of March 1789, and a new one would begin.[17]

2

Federalism and the Tenth Amendment

The Constitutional Convention that authored the United States Constitution we know today was also called "the Federal Convention." When the Constitution was sent to the states for ratification, articles and public letters written under the fake names of "Brutus" and "Cato" began to appear. These articles criticized the proposed strong government.[1] To provide a counterpoint and help convince nervous state governments to approve the new Constitution, James Madison, Alexander Hamilton, and John Jay wrote eighty-five essays under the collective pseudonym of Publius.[2] These pro-Constitution essays became known as "the Federalist Papers,"[3] while the collected Cato and Brutus essays were later called "the Antifederalist Papers."[4]

Ultimately, the "Federalists" won over the "Antifederalists" and the Constitution was ratified. But what were they even arguing about?

What Is Federalism?

In the abstract, federalism is a system that combines a national (federal) government and local, or state, governments. This means determining

In layer cake federalism, state and federal governments have clearly defined roles that do not overlap.

which part of the government has which powers. The two main ways for this interaction between governments to occur are:

Layer cake federalism: This is also called "dual federalism." In layer cake federalism, each government (local, state, federal) has its own clearly defined areas of power that don't overlap, just like the layers in a cake. This is the kind of federalism the United States started with when the Constitution was ratified, up until World War II.[5]

Marble cake federalism: This is also called "cooperative federalism." Imagine a marble cake, with the two different flavors of cake swirled together. There's cooperation and constant interaction between the levels of government in this kind of federalism. For example, state and local governments administer federal programs and regulations. This kind of federalism has been prevalent in the United States since World War II.[6]

The last important piece of American federalism is the second paragraph of Article VI of the Constitution, which reads: "This Constitution, and the laws of the United States which shall be made in pursuance thereof; and all treaties made, or which shall be made, under the authority of the United States, shall be the supreme law of the land; and the judges in every state shall be bound thereby, anything in the Constitution or laws of any State to the contrary notwithstanding." This is often referred to as "the supremacy clause." It means that federal law has precedence over state laws, which is why the national government can challenge state laws in court if they do not comply with federal laws.[7]

The Necessity of the Bill of Rights

The Antifederalist Papers didn't only cause James Madison and Alexander Hamilton to write eighty essays between them. (John Jay only wrote five.) Brutus, Cato, and other Antifederalists also made a convincing argument that the rights and liberties of individuals, such as the right to religious freedom, weren't sufficiently protected by the Constitution as written.[8] Thomas Jefferson, who was not himself an Antifederalist, even wrote in a letter to James Madison that "a bill of rights is what the people are entitled to against every government on earth, general or particular, and what no just government should refuse."[9]

While the Federalists thought that the checks and balances they'd written into the Constitution would be sufficient to prevent oppression by the majority, they also needed to get the constitution ratified. The best way forward was to propose a Bill of Rights be added to the Constitution

after it was ratified, guaranteeing the rights that the Antifederalists were concerned with.[10]

James Madison suggested twelve amendments to the Congress. In the end, ten amendments went to the states for ratification to be added to the Constitution. Those ten amendments specifically limited the powers of the national government. They were called the Bill of Rights. In the 1900s, those rights were extended by courts to limit the power of the states to make laws that trespass on individual liberty, using the due process clause of the Fourteenth Amendment.[11]

"A bill of rights is what the people are entitled to against every government on earth, general or particular, and what no just government should refuse," said Thomas Jefferson.

An amendment is a formal change or addition to an existing document. Articles are part of the original Constitution, whereas amendments were added later.

The Tenth Amendment

The Bill of Rights was intended to limit the powers of the national government, not the states. Because of that, the only amendment of the Bill of Rights that mentions the states at all is the Tenth Amendment, which reads: "The powers not delegated to the United States by the Constitution, nor prohibited by it to the States, are reserved to the States respectively, or to the people."

The Tenth Amendment seems odd next to every other amendment of the Constitution because it doesn't grant or prohibit any rights specifically. It only says that if a power doesn't belong to the national government or

How Is the Constitution Amended?

The amendment process comes from Article V of the Constitution. The men who wrote the document knew it was imperfect and that there needed to be a way to change or fix problems as they arose. They didn't make the process easy. There are two ways for an amendment to be proposed: 1) by a 2/3 majority of both houses of Congress, or 2) by a constitutional convention called by 2/3 of the states. The Constitution has been amended twenty-seven times, and every time the amendment was proposed by Congress. Once an amendment is proposed, 3/4 of the states have to ratify it for it to become part of the Constitution. This process can take years.[12] The longest it's taken an amendment to be ratified is 202 years, 7 months, and 12 days for the 27th amendment.[13]

to individual people, then it belongs to the states. It's somewhat similar to Article II of the outdated Articles of Confederation: "Each state retains its sovereignty, freedom, and independence, and every power, jurisdiction, and right, which is not by this Confederation *expressly* delegated to the United States, in Congress assembled."[14] You notice that the word "expressly" was used in the Articles of Confederation, but not in the Tenth Amendment. The used of the word "expressly" would have been much stronger and clearer language, and it was left out.[15]

In the 1975 case *Fry v. United States*, Justice Douglas wrote:

> *While the Tenth Amendment has been characterized as a "truism," stating merely that "all is retained which has not been surrendered," it is not without significance. The Amendment expressly declares the constitutional policy that Congress may not exercise power in a fashion that impairs the States' integrity or their ability to function effectively in a federal system.*[16]

The Tenth Amendment is mostly used in court to try to limit national laws that interfere with the states, sometimes even when those laws do fall under the powers granted to Congress.[17] States could always make their own laws; that was the intention of the framers of the Constitution, who all had reason to be wary of a national government having too much power. The Constitution and its amendments were there to set the rules about what power the states had to surrender to the national government in order to be part of a bigger country.

3

"States' Rights" and the Civil War

The biggest conflict between state and national governments in the United States was not fought in courtrooms, but on battlefields, in the American Civil War, which lasted from 1861 to 1865. As many as 750,000 people died in that war.[1] However, the war may not have been about "states' rights" in the way you've heard; the claim that the south seceded to protect its sovereignty is a common myth.[2] The main cause of the Civil War was slavery,[3] but what does this have to do with the laws of states versus national laws?

America's "Original Sin"

The Articles of Confederation said nothing about slavery. The articles left the laws regarding the enslavement of abducted African people and their American-born descendants to the states.[4] With the Constitution creating a stronger national government, there was much more for the states to fight over in an attempt to maintain their interests. One point that caused a lot of arguments was about the legislative branch, with the question on whether representation would be equal, with each state having the same number of representatives, or related to population. Small states wanted

The main cause of the Civil War was slavery—between the states that were for it (the Confederacy) and those that were against (the Union).

representation to be equal, and big states wanted it to be proportional; if they had more people, it meant they would have more power in the government.[5]

The "Great Compromise" solved part of the problem: there would be two houses in Congress, one that had equal representation (the Senate) and one that had proportional (the House of Representatives), a split that still has big effects on how our government runs today.[6]

That only opened up a new can of worms, because Southern states had large populations of enslaved people and wanted those people—who were considered property and had no rights—to count toward their populations for determining their number of representatives. Those who opposed the existence of slavery, mostly the Northern states, believed that enslaved people should not be counted at all and should not give the Southern states extra power with their existence. In order to get the Constitution ratified by the Southern states, another compromise was reached, called the "Three-Fifths Compromise." An enslaved person would count as three-fifths of a free (white) person for determining representatives in government.[7]

At the time of the Constitutional Convention, ten states had banned the slave trade. New enslaved people could not be brought to the United

This map shows the United States as it was at the beginning of the Civil War. How many states didn't have slavery?

Legend:
- Union states without slavery
- Union States with slavery
- Confederate States
- Territories

States through those states. The remaining three states—Georgia, North Carolina, and South Carolina—threatened to walk out of the Constitutional Convention if the new Constitution banned the slave trade. Another compromise was made: Congress would have the power to ban the slave trade, but they had to wait until specifically 1808, twenty years after the Constitution was ratified.[8]

The Northwest Ordinance of 1787 had included a clause that people who had escaped their enslavement in those territories were legally required to be returned to their owners. The Southern states were concerned that the five states in the North that had banned slavery and the slave trade (Vermont, New Hampshire, Rhode Island, Connecticut, and Massachusetts) would protect escaped slaves. They insisted that a similar fugitive slave clause be placed in the Constitution.[9]

Slavery was enshrined in the Constitution and set up a battle between the states who wanted slavery abolished and those who wanted to continue to enslave people.

In the Words of South Carolina

The *Declaration of Immediate Causes Which Induce and Justify the Secession of South Carolina from the Federal Union* states, "The General Government, as the common agent, passed laws to carry into effect these stipulations of the States. For many years these laws were executed. But an increasing hostility on the part of the non-slaveholding States to the institution of slavery, has led to a disregard of their obligations, and the laws of the General Government have ceased to effect the objects of the Constitution." The Declaration of Immediate Causes goes on to name laws of the Northern states that have interfered with the Fugitive Slave Acts and states how the national government has failed to enforce its laws.[10]

The Lead-Up to the War Between the States

Despite including the fugitive slave clause in the Constitution, in 1793 Congress passed the Fugitive Slave Act. This was because of pressure from the Southern states. This law was functionally a description of how the fugitive slave clause could be enforced. It allowed slave owners and bounty hunters to hunt for people who had escaped enslavement in the Northern states where slavery had been abolished.[11] Many Northern states refused to enforce this law or passed their own "personal liberty laws" that provided escaped enslaved people trial by jury and lawyers to help them remain free.[12]

In 1842, the Supreme Court decided the case *Prigg v. Pennsylvania* and asserted the supremacy of the Fugitive Slave Act over any state laws that interfered with it.[13] State laws could not overrule the national law.

Eight years later, Southern states pressed Congress to pass the Fugitive Slave Act of 1850. This law placed harsh penalties on federal marshals that refused to enforce the Fugitive Slave Act. It also severely punished free people who helped enslaved people escape.[14] This new law didn't work as intended in the North: it caused more people to become abolitionists and meant more help for escaping enslaved people, and even more personal liberty laws.

During this time, a balance of power between "slave" and "free" states was maintained as new states were admitted to the United States. If a "free" state was admitted, the next state that joined would be a "slave" state. The question of whether or not a new state would allow slavery became increasingly violent. It all came to a head in a conflict known as "Bleeding Kansas." The Kansas-Nebraska Act of 1854 meant that the residents of Kansas would decide if their state would be a free state or a slave state, and Kansas would be the next to join the union. Proslavery and antislavery advocates flooded into Kansas and took up residence to

Abraham Lincoln's election in 1860 prompted South Carolina to secede from the United States. Lincoln believed in the abolishment of slavery.

influence the decision. A violent, miniature civil war took place starting in 1856. Ultimately, Kansas was admitted as a free state in 1861.[15, 16]

These, and more conflicts, culminated in the election of Abraham Lincoln in 1860. Lincoln was a member of the Republican Party, which was largely abolitionist, though in 1860 the party platform only stated that slavery should not spread farther, not that it should be totally abolished.[17, 18] Despite this, Lincoln's election prompted South Carolina to secede from the United States.

In this way, the American Civil War began over slavery, and as a conflict between state and national law. South Carolina was angered into seceding at the federal government's failure to enforce laws supporting the institution of slavery, and Northern states passing laws to oppose it. Ten other states soon followed South Carolina's lead.[19]

4

From Layer Cake to Marble Cake

There isn't an exact date where the US model of federalism switched from the layer cake baked by the framers of the Constitution to the marble cake we have today. The change probably happened because of the New Deal. What was the New Deal and how did it mix the powers of the states and the national government?

The Great Depression and the New Deal

The 1920s in America were a time of massive social and economic change. There was a huge shift in where people lived. For the first time in America's history, more people lived in cities than on farms. This was also the time when American consumer culture really started. There were a lot of new, never-before-seen things for them to buy, like mass-produced clothing, refrigerators, and cars.[1]

Business and the American economy were booming. However, most American workers were not doing as well as the businesses they worked for. Businesses made huge economic gains, with profits growing up to 65 percent from where they had been before the 1920s. Very little of this was shared with workers. Wages had only gone up about 8 percent, and a lot of new consumer goods were bought on credit.[2] This led to a vicious

During the Great Depression, unemployed men came to the
United States Capitol to appeal for federal aid.

cycle of decreased spending, decreased manufacturing due to decreased demand, and increased unemployment.[3] Reckless speculation occurred in the Stock Market on Wall Street. Stocks began to be seriously overvalued. Government policies caused the price for farm goods to drop, rural banks to go bankrupt, and many farmers to lose their land.[4]

On October 24, 1929, investors began to dump overpriced stock shares, causing the value to drop quickly. This became known as "Black Thursday."[5] Bank crashes and an economic depression followed, with massive unemployment. The depression continued for years and may have been extended by national economic policies.[6]

Two and a half years after the Great Depression started, Franklin D. Roosevelt (often called FDR) was selected by the Democratic Party to be their presidential candidate for the election of 1932. In his acceptance speech, FDR said, "I pledge you, I pledge myself, to a new deal for the American people."[7]

After his election, FDR worked to make his new deal a reality. He got the Congress to pass two wide-ranging packages of "New Deal" bills that included bank reforms, aid packages for business and struggling people, work programs, and controls on things like how much farm goods had to be bought for. Many programs that still exist today like Social Security and unemployment protection came from the New Deal.[8]

Was the New Deal Constitutional?

Until 1937, the Supreme Court ruled that almost every New Deal law that was challenged by states and businesses was actually unconstitutional. The government tried to argue that the programs fell under the commerce and

Sick Chickens Versus the New Deal

Before the "switch in time that saved the nine," there was A.L.A. *Schechter Poultry Corp. v. United States*, also known as the "sick chicken case."[9] Under new regulations created by the National Industrial Recovery Act (NIRA), Schechter Poultry was charged with multiple counts of "the sale to a butcher of an unfit chicken," as well as violations of minimum wage laws. The case went all the way to the Supreme Court, which decided that NIRA was an unconstitutional violation of the separation of powers in the Constitution because the regulations were viewed as Congress giving legislative power to the executive branch.[10] NIRA was important to the New Deal, and the "sick chicken case" was one of the reasons FDR began to look at packing the court as a solution.[11]

taxation clauses of the Constitution, but the court felt that those powers did not cover industrial regulation or social and economic reforms.[12–14]

Frustrated, FDR and his allies in Congress hatched a plan to change the makeup of the Supreme Court to something friendlier toward their policies. Legislation was introduced to add a new justice to the Supreme Court for every current justice over the age of seventy. This would have allowed FDR to pack the court with liberal justices who would have agreed New Deal laws were constitutional.

Franklin Roosevelt worked to write a New Deal for the American People in an effort to end the Great Depression. Social Security was one such New Deal program.

The next case after this legislation was announced, *West Coast Hotel v. Parrish*, was decided in favor of the government. Shortly after, one of the conservative justices also retired, and the "court packing" legislation fizzled out because it was no longer needed.[15] This seeming change to the Supreme Court's attitude on the New Deal became known as "the switch in time that saved the nine,"[16] because it preserved the court's size at nine justices.

Justice Felix Frankfurter later issued a memo to say that the threatened legislation had no influence on how the court decided *West Coast Hotel v. Parrish*.[17] After that case, the New Deal laws were found constitutional and the power of the federal government expanded into new areas, including the layers of regulations we know today.

The Supreme Court of the United States is the highest court in the country. The court has jurisdiction over lawsuits between two states.

The New Deal made the federal government much larger and gave it a much more active role in society through its new programs. It began the trend of state and local governments becoming involved in the administration of federal programs, often at the insistence of those governments.[18] The New Deal also marked the beginning of the system of federal regulations used to enforce laws[19] that we have today. These regulations interact with and can challenge state laws.[20] This mixing of executive power created the marble cake federalism we are familiar with today.

5

Federalism Today

The United States has long since passed the layer cake federalism the original framers of the Constitution created. What we have today might be marble cake federalism or another kind that future historians will give a delicious-sounding name to. But what does this mean for state laws and federal laws? How do the layers of laws affect our every-day lives, and how does the enforcement of federal laws interact with state laws?

Federal Mandates, State Laws

The national government can sometimes force states to make laws by mandating it. A federal mandate is a law, regulation, or court decision made by the federal government that compels state or local governments—or businesses—to create programs or make laws of their own to comply with the law. There can be punishments for the states if they don't comply.[1] Unfunded mandates are those where there are significant costs to the states, and the federal government doesn't provide money to help.[2]

A recent example of a mandate is the No Child Left Behind Act, which required that all schools receiving federal funds undertake standardized testing developed by their states. Schools could lose their federal funding or even be closed if students did not show "adequate yearly progress" after interventions.[3] No Child Left Behind was thought by many to be an unfunded mandate, since no money was given by the government to help with the cost of testing or development of standards. Several school districts attempted to sue the federal government over this, but the Supreme Court decided not to hear the case in 2010. SCOTUS preserved a lower court ruling that said No Child Left Behind wasn't an unfunded mandate.[4] The most controversial parts of No Child Left Behind were changed by the Every Student Succeeds Act, signed by President Obama in 2015.[5]

To Enforce, or Not to Enforce?

Sometimes state laws conflict with federal laws, and the federal government decides to not sue or otherwise use its enforcement powers. States can effectively "break" federal laws, and the federal government allows it.

Marijuana is illegal in the United States under the Controlled Substances Act (CSA), which means that people can be punished for buying, selling, or growing it.[6] However, since 1996, over thirty states have legalized the use of marijuana in some form for medical reasons, and a smaller subset allows it to be sold for recreation.[7]

In 2013, Deputy Attorney General James M. Cole wrote a memo to give enforcement guidance about marijuana to his department. In it, he says that the federal government won't enforce the CSA in states that have legalized marijuana, with a few exceptions for priorities like preventing money from the sale of marijuana going to drug cartels.[8] This effectively gave permission to the states to create and enforce their own laws, even though marijuana was still technically illegal under the CSA. In 2018, Attorney General Jeff Sessions rescinded Cole's memo, which has left the states with legal marijuana uncertain how or when the federal government may start enforcing the CSA again.[9]

President George W. Bush signs the No Child Left Behind Act into law.

The Regulatory State

On September 30, 2018, California passed a bill into law that enforces "net neutrality" in the state. California's law says that internet providers cannot selectively slow or block specific kinds of content or charge companies more money for better access for their customers. Within hours of the law being passed, the federal government sued California.[10, 11]

Under President Obama, net neutrality was guaranteed federally, but it wasn't because of a law. It was because President Obama pushed the Federal Communications Commission (FCC) to classify internet service as a telecommunication service under the Communications Act of 1934. This meant that it would have to be neutral under the federal laws that regulated telephones.[12] Under President Trump, at the end of 2017, the FCC repealed these regulations and federal net neutrality ended.[13]

Net neutrality at the federal level was determined entirely by regulations. Congress could pass a law that explicitly states that the internet must be neutral but has not. What are regulations, and why are they so much easier to change than laws?

After Congress passes a law and the president signs it, the law needs to be enforced. Laws often aren't created with the details of *how* they should be followed. An environmental law might not say how much of a kind of

Federal Law Enforcement

Everyone knows about the Federal Bureau of Investigation (FBI) and the US Marshals, both of which fall under the Department of Justice. But most of the departments of the federal government have their own law enforcement arm, which makes certain that federal laws and regulations are followed. Here are three examples:

Department of Agriculture—The Forest Service Law Enforcement and Investigations officers protect natural resources and national park visitors, and sometimes get around on boats, snowmobiles, or dirt bikes.

Department of the Interior—National Park Service Rangers work to enforce good land stewardship.

Department of Energy—Office of Secure Transportation agents see to the safe movement of nuclear weapons across America by road and other means.

pollutant is illegal—it's up to the agency in charge of the law, in this case the Environmental Protection Agency (EPA), to create a regulation that defines what is illegal. First the EPA proposes the rule and opens it to public comment. Then it issues the final rule, which is then written into the Code of Federal Regulations. Then it is up to the EPA to enforce that brand new regulation.[14]

If state and federal law come into conflict, state and federal governments can sue each other. Then it's up to the courts to decide if the federal

Net neutrality ensures that the internet is treated equally everywhere and that no internet provider can slow, censor, or otherwise curtail the content its customers access.

Marijuana is becoming legal for both medical and recreational purposes in specific states, but it remains largely illegal at a federal level.

government had the power to make the law that the regulation falls under, or if the power belongs to the state.

Sometimes the federal government wins, such as when the Supreme Court forced desegregation of schools in states with *Brown v. Board of Education*. Sometimes the state government wins, such as when state governments forced the federal government to recognize same-sex marriage with *United States v. Windsor*.

The relationship between the federal government and states is still in flux and will be as long as our laws and our understanding of the Constitution that is their foundation continue to evolve.

Chapter Notes

Introduction

1. "Marriage Law and Legal Definition," USLegal.com, https://definitions.uslegal.com/m/marriage/.

2. "The Defense of Marriage Act (DOMA) and the Call for a Constitutional Convention," FindLaw.com, https://family.findlaw.com/marriage/the-defense-of-marriage-act-and-the-call-for-a-constitutional.html.

3. "Same-Sex Couple Ties the Knot at Midnight," *VPR*, September 1, 2009, https://vprarchive.vpr.net/vpr-news/same-sex-couple-ties-the-knot-at-midnight/.

4. Ibid.

5. Bill Clinton, "Bill Clinton: It's time to overturn DOMA," *Washington Post*, March 7, 2013, https://www.washingtonpost.com/opinions/bill-clinton-its-time-to-overturn-doma/2013/03/07/fc184408-8747-11e2-98a3-b3db6b9ac586_story.html.

6. *Massachusetts v. Department of Health and Human Services*, 1:09-cv-11156-JLT, Justia.com, https://cases.justia.com/federal/district-courts/massachusetts/madce/1:2009cv11156/123233/58/0.pdf.

7. *Gill v. Office of Personnel Management*, 1:09-cv-10309-JLT, Justia.com, https://cases.justia.com/federal/district-courts/massachusetts/madce/1:2009cv10309/120672/70/0.pdf.

8. *United States v. Windsor*, 570 US 744 (2013), Justia.com, https://supreme.justia.com/cases/federal/us/570/12-307/.

9. Ibid.

10. Ibid.

11. "Federal Court Rules DOMA Sec. 3 Violates Equal Protection," *Poliglot* (accessed via archive.org), July 8, 2010, https://web.archive.org/web/20100712061020/http://www.metroweekly.com/poliglot/2010/07/federal-court-rules-doma-viola.html.

12. "The Bill of Rights: A Transcription," National Archives, https://www.archives.gov/founding-docs/bill-of-rights-transcript#toc-amendment-x.

13. "Tenth Amendment," Annenberg Classroom, http://www.annenbergclassroom.org/page/tenth-amendment.

14. "State-by-State History of Banning and Legalizing Gay Marriage, 1994-2015," ProCon.org, February 16, 2016, https://gaymarriage.procon.org/view.resource.php?resourceID=004857.

Chapter One: The Need for a Constitution

1. "Articles of Confederation 1777-1781," Office of the Historian, https://history.state.gov /milestones/1776-1783/articles.

2. "Articles of Confederation," Britannica.com, https://www.britannica.com/topic /Articles-of-Confederation.

3. "Albany Plan of Union, 1754," Office of the Historian, https://history.state.gov /milestones/1750-1775/albany-plan.

4. "Articles of Confederation," History.com, https://www.history.com/topics/early-us /articles-of-confederation.

5. Donald Applestein, Esq., "The Road to Union: America's forgotten first constitution," May 14, 2014, https://www.sesp.northwestern.edu/msed/files/pdfs/theory-practice /National%20Constitution%20Center%20Blog.pdf.

6. "The Three-Fifths Compromise," Digital History, http://www.digitalhistory.uh.edu /disp_textbook.cfm?smtid=3&psid=163.

7. "Supremacy Clause," Legal Information Institute, https://www.law.cornell.edu/wex /supremacy_clause.

8. "The Articles of Confederation and Perpetual Union – 1777," UShistory.org, http://www .ushistory.org/documents/confederation.htm.

9. Ibid.

10. "Articles of Confederation," Digital History, http://www.digitalhistory.uh.edu/disp_text book.cfm?smtid=2&psid=3225.

11. "The Pennsylvania Line Mutiny," social.rollins.edu, September 25, 2012, http://social .rollins.edu/wpsites/hist120/2012/09/25/pennsylvania-line-mutiny/.

12. "The Northwest Ordinance of 1787," History, Art & Archives of the United States House of Representatives, http://history.house.gov/Historical-Highlights/1700s /Northwest-Ordinance-1787/.

13. "Northwest Ordinance (1787)," ourdocuments.gov, https://www.ourdocuments.gov /doc.php?flash=false&doc=8.

14. Ibid.

15. Eric P. Newman, *The Early Paper Money of America* (Iola, WI: Krause Publications, 1990).

16. Ibid.

17. "By the United States in Congress Assembled," Library of Congress, https://www.loc .gov/resource/bdsdcc.2410h.

Chapter Two: Federalism and the Tenth Amendment

1. "The Constitutional Convention Debates and the Anti-Federalist Papers," American History from Revolution to Reconstruction and Beyond, http://www.let.rug.nl/usa /documents/1786-1800/the-anti-federalist-papers/.

2. Gordon Lloyd, "Introduction to the Federalist," TeachingAmericanHistory.org, http:// teachingamericanhistory.org/ratification/federalist/.

3. "The Federalist: A collection of essays, written in favor of the new Constitution, as agreed upon by the Federal Convention, September 17, 1787," Library of Congress, https://www .loc.gov/resource/rbc0001.2014jeff21562v1/?sp=11&r=-1.843,-0.06,4.685,1.745,0.

4. Ibid.

5. "History of Federalism," SparkNotes, https://www.sparknotes.com /us-government-and-politics/american-government/federalism/section2/page/2/.

6. "Concepts of Federalism," CliffsNotes, https://www.cliffsnotes.com/study-guides /american-government/federalism/concepts-of-federalism.

7. "Bill of Rights," Britannica.com, https://www.britannica.com/topic/Bill -of-Rights-United-States-Constitution.

8. "The Bill of Rights: A Brief History," ACLU.org, https://www.aclu.org/other /bill-rights-brief-history.

9. "The Bill of Rights: Its History and Significance," *Exploring Constitutional Conflicts*, http://law2.umkc.edu/faculty/projects/ftrials/conlaw/billofrightsintro.html.

10. Ibid.

11. "Constitutional Amendment Process," National Archives, https://www.archives.gov /federal-register/constitution.

12. "The Constitution: Anecdotal Amendment Factoids," LexisNexis.com, http://www .lexisnexis.com/constitution/amendments_factoids.asp.

13. "Articles of Confederation: March 1, 1781," the Avalon Project, http://avalon.law.yale .edu/18th_century/artconf.asp.

14. "Reserved Powers," Legal Information Institute, https://www.law.cornell.edu /constitution-conan/amendment-10/reserved-powers.

15. *Fry v. United States*, 421 US 542 (1975), findlaw.com, https://caselaw.findlaw.com /us-supreme-court/421/542.html.

16. Ibid.

17. Ibid.

Chapter Three: "States' Rights" and the Civil War

1. "New Estimate Raises Civil War Death Toll," *New York Times*, April 2, 2012, https://www .nytimes.com/2012/04/03/science/civil-war-toll-up-by-20-percent-in-new-estimate.html.

2. James W. Loewen, "Five Myths About Why the South Seceded," *Washington Post*, February 26, 2011, https://www.washingtonpost.com/outlook/five-myths-about-why -the-south-seceded/2011/01/03/ABHr6jD_story.html?utm_term=.4eb92cbc5d26.

3. Ta-Nehisi Coates, "What This Cruel War Was Over," *Atlantic*, June 22, 2015, https:// www.theatlantic.com/politics/archive/2015/06/what-this-cruel-war-was-over/396482/.

4. "The Constitution and Slavery," Constitutional Right Foundation, http://www.crf-usa .org/black-history-month/the-constitution-and-slavery.

5. Ibid.

6. Amanda Onion, "How the Great Compromise Affects Politics Today," History.com, April 17, 2018, https://www.history.com/news/how-the-great-compromise-affects-politics-today.

7. "The Three-Fifths Compromise," Digital History, http://www.digitalhistory.uh.edu /disp_textbook.cfm?smtid=3&psid=163.

8. Ibid.

9. "Fugitive Slave Acts," History.com, https://www.history.com/topics/black-history /fugitive-slave-acts.

10. "Confederate States of America – Decalaration of Immediate Causes Which Induce and Justify the Secession of South Carolina from the Federal Union," the Avalon Project, http://avalon.law.yale.edu/19th_century/csa_scarsec.asp.

11. "Fugitive Slave Acts," History.com.

12. "Personal-Liberty Laws," Britannica.com, https://www.britannica.com/topic /personal-liberty-laws.

13. *Prigg v. Pennsylvania*, 41 US 539 (1842), Oyez.org, https://www.oyez.org /cases/1789-1850/41us539.

14. "Fugitive Slave Acts," Britannica.com, https://www.britannica.com/event /Fugitive-Slave-Acts.

15. "Bleeding Kansas," Britannica.com, https://www.britannica.com/event /Bleeding-Kansas-United-States-history.

16. "Bleeding Kansas," History.com, https://www.history.com/topics/19th-century /bleeding-kansas.

17. United States Presidential Election of 1860," Britannica.com, https://www.britannica.com/event/United-States-presidential-election-of-1860.

18. "Election of 1860," mtholyoke.edu, https://www.mtholyoke.edu/~ewdow/Politics%20116/electionof1860-2.html.

19. "Declaration of Causes of Seceding States," Battlefields.org, https://www.battlefields.org/learn/primary-sources/declaration-causes-seceding-states.

Chapter Four: From Layer Cake to Marble Cake

1. "The Roaring Twenties History," History.com, https://www.history.com/topics/roaring-twenties/roaring-twenties-history.

2. "The Great Depression," PBS.org, https://www.pbs.org/wgbh/americanexperience/features/dustbowl-great-depression/.

3. Ibid.

4. "Great Depression and Herbert Hoover," Iowa Department of Cultural Affairs, https://iowaculture.gov/history/education/educator-resources/primary-source-sets/great-depression-and-herbert-hoover.

5. "Black Thursday," InvestingAnswers.com, https://investinganswers.com/financial-dictionary/stock-market/black-thursday-915.

6. Lee E. Ohanian "Why Did the Great Depression Last So Long?" *Forbes*, https://www.forbes.com/2009/04/30/1930s-labor-wages-business-ohanian.html#712a9ce17b1c.

7. "Great Depression and World War II, 1929–1945," Library of Congress, http://www.loc.gov/teachers/classroommaterials/presentationsandactivities/presentations/timeline/depwwii/newdeal/.

8. "New Deal," Britannica.com, https://www.britannica.com/event/New-Deal.

9. "Schechter Poultry Corp. v. United States," Britannica.com, https://www.britannica.com/event/Schechter-Poultry-Corp-v-United-States.

10. *A.L.A. Schechter Poultry Corp. v. United States*, 295 US 495 (1935), Justia.com, https://supreme.justia.com/cases/federal/us/295/495/.

11. Ibid.

12. Ibid.

13. John Hardman, "The Great Depression and the New Deal," EDGE, https://web.stanford.edu/class/e297c/poverty_prejudice/soc_sec/hgreat.htm.

14. K. J. Johnson, "Was the New Deal a Constitutional Revolution?" USHI Module, http://academic.brooklyn.cuny.edu/history/johnson/ushinewdeal.htm.

15. Ibid.

16. "When a Switch in Time Saved Nine," *New York Times*, November 10, 1985, https://www.nytimes.com/1985/11/10/opinion/l-when-a-switch-in-time-saved-nine-143165.html.

17. "'Mr. Justice Roberts,' by Felix Frankfurter, December 1955," Arthur J. Morris Law Library, http://archives.law.virginia.edu/records/mss/86-5/digital/2940.

18. Michael D. Bordo, Claudia Goldin, and Eugene N. White, *The Defining Moment: The Great Depression and the American Economy in the Twentieth Century* (Chicago, IL: University of Chicago Press, 1998). Accessed via: http://www.nber.org/chapters/c6892.pdf.

19. "The Basics of the Regulatory Process," EPA.gov, https://www.epa.gov/laws-regulations/basics-regulatory-process.

20. Cass R. Sunstein, "The Constitution after the New Deal," *Harvard Law Review*, vol. 101 no. 2, December 1987. Accessed via: https://www.jstor.org/stable/1341264?seq=1#page_scan_tab_contents.

Chapter Five: Federalism Today

1. Catherine H. Lovell, Max Neiman, Robert Kneisel, Adam Rose, and Charele Tobin, *Federal and State Mandating on Local Governments: Report to the National Science Foundation* (Riverside, CA: University of California, 1979).

2. "Unfunded Mandate," BusinessDictionary.com, http://www.businessdictionary.com/definition/unfunded-mandate.html.

3. "Adequate Yearly Progess," *Education Week*, July 18, 2011, https://www.edweek.org/ew/issues/adequate-yearly-progress/index.html.

4. "NEA Disappointed in Supreme Court's Decision to Deny Review of Unfunded Mandate Case," National Education Association, http://www.nea.org/archive/39787.htm.

5. "President Obama Signs into Law a Rewrite of No Child Left Behind," *New York Times*, December 10, 2015, https://www.nytimes.com/2015/12/11/us/politics/president-obama-signs-into-law-a-rewrite-of-no-child-left-behind.html.

6. "Federal Marijuana Law," Americans for Safe Access, https://www.safeaccessnow.org/federal_marijuana_law.

7. "The State-by-State Guide to Weed in America," *Rolling Stone*, https://www.rollingstone.com/culture/culture-news/the-state-by-state-guide-to-weed-in-america-627968/.

8. James M. Cole, "Memorandum for All United States Attorneys," August 29, 2013. Accessed via: https://www.justice.gov/iso/opa/resources/3052013829132756857467.pdf.

9. "Sessions Nixes Obama Rules Leaving States Alone That Legalize Pot," CNN, January 4, 2018, https://www.cnn.com/2018/01/04/politics/jeff-sessions-cole-memo/index.html.

10. "California Just Passed Its Net Neutrality Law. The DOJ Is Already Suing," CNN Business, September 30, 2018, https://money.cnn.com/2018/09/30/technology/california-net -neutrality-law/index.html.

11. "Justice Department Sues California Over Net Neutrality Law," NPR, October 2, 2018, https://www.npr.org/2018/10/02/653570076/justice-department-sues -california-over-net-neutrality-law.

12. "Obama Asks F.C.C. to Adopt Tough Net Neutrality Rules," *New York Times*, November 10, 2014, https://www.nytimes.com/2014/11/11/technology/obama-net-neutrality-fcc.html.

13. "The End of Net Neutrality Is Here," CNN Business, June 10, 2018, https://money.cnn .com/2018/06/10/technology/net-neutrality/index.html.

14. "The Basics of the Regulatory Process," EPA.gov, https://www.epa.gov/laws-regulations /basics-regulatory-process.

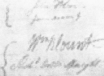

Glossary

abolitionists Before the American Civil War, people who wanted to end the institution of slavery.

Antifederalists During the formation of the United States government, people who opposed the creation of a strong central government in general. Antifederalists opposed the Constitutional Convention of 1787, preferring the weak government of the Articles of Confederation.

depreciation The decrease in value of some asset, such as land or money, over time.

federalism A form of government in which there is a division of power between a national government and smaller regional governments.

Federalists During the formation of the United States government, people who believed that the central government should be strong and have power over the state governments.

layer cake federalism A kind of federalism in which national and state government powers are distinct, separate, and do not overlap. This type of federalism generally existed in the United States before the New Deal.

marble cake federalism A kind of federalism in which the powers of national and state government overlap. For example, state governments administering national programs. This type of federalism has generally existed in the United States since the New Deal.

mutiny Rebellion against proper authority, normally soldiers or sailors against their commanding officers.

ratification Signing or giving formal consent for a legal document or treaty. The United States Constitution had to be ratified by the states before it could go into effect.

regulations Rules made by agencies in the executive branch of the government to define how laws should be applied. More generally, a rule made by any government body that has the force of law.

secede To formally withdraw from a federal union or other organization. The Southern states left the United States by seceding, setting off the Civil War.

sovereign A state or nation having supreme, independent power.

speculation Purchasing an asset, such as stocks, at great risk of loss in the hopes that they will instead gain value.

truism A statement that is obviously true.

unfunded mandate A law or judicial decision that compels state governments or others to act but does not provide the money that is necessary for the compelled changes to be made.

Further Reading

Books

Kanefield, Teri. *Alexander Hamilton: The Making of America*. New York, NY: Harry N. Abrams, 2018.

Levinson, Cynthia. *Fault Lines in the Constitution: The Framers, Their Fights, and the Flaws that Affect Us Today*. Atlanta, GA: Peachtree Publishers, 2017.

Miranda, Lin-Manuel. *Hamilton: The Revolution*. New York, NY: Grand Central Publishing, 2016.

Rothman, Lily. *Everything You Need to Ace American History in One Big Fat Notebook*. New York, NY: Workman Publishing, 2016.

Websites

The Crash Course

thecrashcourse.com/courses/ushistory

John and Hank Green publish accessible and fun videos about American history.

Our Documents

ourdocuments.gov

A site created by the National Initiative on American History, with pictures of many original documents that are important to our history and their significance explained.

Teaching American History

teachingamericanhistory.org

A site with documents and online exhibits about the history of America.

Index